The Reiki I Handbook

A guide for Reiki I students

Hannah Edwards

Reiki I Handbook: A guide for Reiki I students

ISBN: 978 1 4452 0073 6

www.reiki-with-hannah.co.uk

Table of Contents

Introduction

What is Reiki?

Reiki (pronounced 'ray-key') is the name given to both the system of healing developed by Mikao Usui in the late 19th century and the energy that flows through it.

The word Reiki is composed of two Japanese words (pictured right):

Rei - Meaning 'universal'
Ki - meaning 'energy'

So Reiki is a universal flow of energy. It has been described in many ways, from a neutral force of nature, a specific range of natural vibrations, even the outpouring of the love of God and it is known and worked with in many cultures under many different names (such as *chi, prana* and *spirit.*)

Is Reiki a religion?

Although the outer form of Reiki owes much to the Tendai Buddhism of its founder, Mikao Usui, Reiki is not religious in nature and requires no particular beliefs. Today Reiki is practiced by people of many different faiths and those with no formal religious ties.

How does it compare to other energy work?

The practice of Reiki is both similar to and different from other types of energy work such as Spiritual Healing and Chakra Cleansing. We're all using the same source, the universal energy, but there are three main defining elements of healing in the Reiki tradition which make it distinct from other types of energy work:

- The use of Attunments to initiate the Reiki practitioner
- The use of specific symbols from the second degree onward
- The use of intuition rather than pattern to guide the course of healing.

Reiki healing is generally found to be simpler to study and more direct in its methods than other types of energy healing.

How can I work with Reiki?

Anyone who has been attuned to Reiki can channel[1] the energy through their hands, gaze and even breath.

Energy begins to flow when an attuned person connects with the energy and sets their intention to heal. Once you have received the Reiki I attunements you are immediately able to channel Reiki with your intention.

However, you can do more if you want to become an effective healer for yourself and others and we'll cover the level I aspects in this book.

It is sometimes said that Reiki is always working to the highest good so it doesn't really matter where you put your hands or what you do with your mind when you're using Reiki. Some Reiki practitioners will even chat or plan their route home when giving treatments. I'd really like you to engage with the energy more than that!

In the beginning stages of learning Reiki you will need to consciously work with the energy, using it intelligently and sensitively if you're going to understand the feedback you're getting from your hands and the sensations you're encountering as you work on yourself and others. In time you'll find that your intuition and practice combine to create a more effortless practice, flowing and graceful, but until then we've got some work to do.

I'd encourage you to use the practices outlined in the sections on *Becoming a hollow bamboo* and *Helpful practices* to aid you in this.

---

[1] When I use the word 'channel' in this handbook I'm referring to the ability to let Reiki pass through you unimpeded, NOT to the practice of receiving information from spirit guides, deities or other sources.

The Reiki Principles

You may have heard of the Reiki Principles or Precepts, the five intentions that the founder of Reiki gave us as a basis for a strong Reiki practice:

Just for today...

I will not be angry
I will not worry
I will be grateful
I will work honestly
I will be kind to every living thing

Although we have already said that Reiki is not a religious system it has a strong moral and spiritual dimension to it and the Reiki Principles are the key to understanding that aspect of our discipline.

Mikao Usui, referred to hereafter as Usui-sensei, envisioned the Reiki approach to life as one of personal spiritual growth leading to greater healing abilities and increased happiness. If we live by the Principles we begin to cultivate the kind of mind and spirit that are free from negative vibrations, that are sensitive enough to tune into the healing energies and are open enough to share our gifts with others.

As you'll no doubt discover it's hard to concentrate on healing when you've got angry thoughts, nagging worries or meanness pulling at your mind. A commitment to the Principles won't magically free you from these distractions but over time, as you try to live out that commitment, you'll begin to notice that you don't need, and are actually harmed by, these negative emotions and that you are freed and lightened when practicing the positive ones. When coupled with the meditative practices later in this book you'll find that the Principles increase your ability to free-up your mind and let it experience its basic, positive state. This is the state most conducive to healing, where energy can flow unimpeded and you are most receptive to all the energy has to tell you.

The three degrees of Reiki

In Western Reiki there are three degrees or levels forming a progression in healing from:

- the body and and your immediate environment
- to the mind, emotions and those distant in time and space
- to the soul or spirt and transmitting Reiki to others.

First degree - *Shoden*
You are now at the first stage of this journey, opening yourself up the healing energy so that you can relieve the problems of the physical body. This is not to say that emotional healing can't be brought about by Reiki practice at the Shoden level, it can, but the main focus here is on physical healing.

Second degree - *Okuden*
At the second level Reiki practitioners receive the first three symbols that allow them to:
- intensify their physical healing
- heal mental and emotional wounds
- transmit Reiki over distances

This is the minimum level if you wish to be a professional Reiki practitioner and charge for treatments.

Third Degree - *Shinpiden*
At the third and final degree you receive the final symbol and are instructed in the attunement process so that you can attune students of your own.

Some Reiki teachers split this level into two sections, the first granting you just the title of Reiki master and the second giving you teaching status.

The History of Reiki

There have been many competing histories of Reiki, mainly stemming from an early desire to make Reiki more acceptable to a Western audience by claiming a wishful semi-Christian heritage for its founder Mikao Usui.

However, in recent years there has been a more through investigation of the roots of Reiki and the following outline appears to be the most reliable story we have so far:

Mikao Usui

Reiki began with a Japanese man called Mikao Usui (b.15/8/1865 d.9/3/1926).

Much of his life is lost in the tangle of competing stories told about him by different Reiki masters, but Usui-sensei is known to have worked as private secretary to a politician and to have later founded his own business, but so far there is no evidence as to its nature.

His memorial stone tells us that he was always interested in spiritual things and we know that he taught a method of hands-on-healing and spiritual development before his famous *satori* (flash of enlightenment) on Mt. Kurama which lead to the creation of Reiki as we know it.

The *satori* took place towards the end of his life during a traditional twenty-one day retreat on mt. Kurama, one of five he made in his lifetime. On the final day of the retreat, deep in meditation, he felt a sudden rush of energy through the top of his head and an intuition about how to use it. He began to use the energy to treat himself, his friends and family members and in 1922 opened a clinic in order to help others.

Both Usui and Reiki became famous in Japan following the 1923 earthquake that devastated Tokyo and Yokohama. Usui went out onto the streets to successfully treat the injured and, according to his memorial stone, "reached out his hands of love to suffering people".

It has become apparent as investigations continue that the Reiki taught by Usui-sensei was of the gentle intuitive kind with an emphasis on personal spiritual growth, regular meditation and compassionate moral values. Much of this approach had been lost in the West through an emphasis on more rigid, systematic approaches such as set hand positions, fixed fees for teaching and a lack of spiritual training. This deficit is being addressed now through the pioneering work of Western Reiki practitioners such as Frank Arjava Petter who have gone to Japan and sought out the original sources of Reiki.

So why is the Western system so very different from the Eastern source? The drift into formalism seems to have begun with a Japanese medical doctor, a student of Usui-sensei's who wanted a more organised and easily teachable form of Reiki to use in clinical practice...

Dr. Chujiro Hayashi

Dr Hayashi (b.15/9/1878 d.10/5/1940) was a very different type of man to Mikao Usui. As a doctor in the Imperial Navy and a Christian he was more interested in the physical healing aspects of Usui's teachings than the spiritual aspects and personal growth.

Having been trained by Usui-sensei during the last 10 months of his life Dr Hayashi remained in the society formed to carry on Usui-sensei's work, the *Usui Reiki Ryoho Gakkai,* until 1931 when he left to open his own clinic.

Over time Dr Hayashi changed the traditional method of training Reiki students from that of regular meetings coupled with months and years of practice to one of specific training courses with set curriculums and short time frames. This is the kind of Reiki that our next landmark figure in Western Reiki would study and eventually bring to the West.

Hawayo Takata

Mrs Hawayo Takata (b.1900 d.1980) came from her birth place in Hawaii to Dr. Hayashi's clinic suffering from a tumor. Although skeptical at first she became convinced when she when she found herself completely healed and she decided to study Reiki.

She attained the Master level in 1938 and was given permission to teach in the west by Dr. Hayashi. She returned to Hawaii and opened a clinic and Reiki school, training twenty-two Reiki masters, including her granddaughter Phyllis Lei Furumoto, before her death in 1980.

Most Western Reiki practitioners still have Mrs Takata in their lineage and she is widely credited as the original source of Western Reiki. No other practitioners in either the *Gakkai* or the Hayashi line are known to have taught outside of Japan.

However, for all of her virtues Mrs Takata remains a highly controversial figure in the Reiki community. As the true history of the main Reiki figures comes to light it also becomes clear that Mrs Takata invented what she thought was a more palatable story for her Western students. She changed Mikao Usui from a layman and committed Tendai Buddhist into a medical doctor and Christian monk who travelled the world in search of the true origin of the miracles of Jesus. This story is completely apocryphal but is still told in many Reiki classes even now.

The origin of the fabled $10,000 fee for Reiki mastership also rests with Mrs Takata. She charged this amount throughout her life for mastership training and urged her students to do the same. This was based on her principle of 'the exchange of gifts': as Reiki was precious it could only be fully realised and appreciated if the student paid a very high price for it. This inhibited the early growth of Reiki, which Usui-sensei had specifically stated was for everyone, and brought an unhealthy financial element into the teaching early on.

With these and other revelations in mind some modern masters seek to entirely circumvent the teachings of Mrs Takata and return to a more authentic form of Reiki, claiming that this source is tainted. Others feel that Reiki has been accurately transmitted by Mrs Takata in all its essential elements and that Japanese and Western styles are simply different expressions of the same energy.

In the end it's clear to everyone who's been attuned or had *Reiju* that everyone, whether of Eastern or Western lineages and styles, can channel Reiki effectively. It is sad and regrettable that most Western Reiki people have been taught a fiction about the founder of their discipline, but we still received the gift of Reiki and the truth will come to light in the end if we give it time.

Reiki today

Today there are many styles of Reiki, with people's inclinations tending them towards a particular one, either more or less mystical in presentation, more or less demanding terms of time and money, more grounded in a particular culture (Japanese, Celtic, Tibetan, Egyptian etc.) Some practitioners even choose to study in several different lineages.

The style of Reiki I teach on my courses and that you learned in class is usually called Usui Reiki, although that's not a very satisfactory name. The emphasis is on both personal growth, through the Reiki Principles and meditation, and on intuitive hands-on healing. I teach original Japanese energy techniques as well as the traditional Western hand positions so that you have a comprehensive overview of the possibilities at this level of training.

If you'd like more detailed information about the origins of Reiki there is an annotated book list at the back of this guide.

Attunements

What is an attunement?

An attunement is a ritual in which a Reiki master works with your energy field to connect you with the universal energy flow and help open you as a channel for the energy.

The ritual involves:
- **movement**, with the Reiki master circling your chair,
- **touch**, with the Reiki master laying their hand on your shoulders and tapping your palms.
- **symbols**, which are impressed on your energy centres and
- **breath**, with the Reiki master blowing the symbols into your aura.

Some students find this a calming process leading to deeper relaxation bringing a great deal of comfort and healing, however for others attunements can also be times of release. It is not unusual for students to burst into tears during an attunement and this is also to be welcomed as it brings its own form of cleansing with it. Do not be embarrassed if this happens to you.

A third effect of the awakening energy maybe sensations of heat, tingling or vibration in the body with or without images, colours and sounds in the mind. These effects are also to be welcomed as an expression of your opening to new energies. Whatever your experiences with the energy, they will be ultimately beneficial to you.

During the Reiki I level you will experience four attunements. At the end of the last attunement you will open your eyes as a Reiki I practitioner.

What about *Reiju* empowerments?

You may have heard of an alternative way to connect you to the energy called a *Reiju* empowerment or *Reiju* blessing. This is an older more authentic form of the connection ritual which was used by Usui-sensei on all his students. It is shorter and it doesn't use the Reiki symbols.

In the transmission of Reiki to the West this original ritual, with its roots in buddhist blessings, has elongated and changed into the symbol based attunement ritual that we have now and has only recently returned to Western practice.

There is no real consensus in Reiki circles as whether we should return to Usui-sensei's original practice and abandon the Western attunements or whether the attunements are a vital development in the system and help you to work with symbols later on. Several well known Reiki masters take very definite stands on either side of the argument and students from both sides have been upset when their form of initiation was called either 'weak' or 'inauthentic' by people of the opposite view.

In order to sidestep this issue I use the standard Western attunement as my basic connection ritual but offer at least one *Reiju* empowerment to all students attending my courses and at all the Reiki shares I run. If you have a preference for *Reiju* then I'll be happy to replace one, two, three or all of your attunements with an empowerment.

My personal view is that both *Reiju* empowerments and Western attunements work equally well and confer all the same benefits, even when working with symbols. My tastes run to the *Reiju* empowerment as the more authentic and beautiful form but I wouldn't put it any more strongly than that.

The effects of attunements

Once the last attunement or empowerment is over you are truly a novice Reiki practitioner. You have the ability to heal yourself and others and your ability to channel the energy doesn't decay or recede with time.

Your energy has been permanently changed to allow Reiki to flow through you and now when you place your hands on yourself or someone else with the intention to heal, you become a channel for the healing energy.

What will I feel?

Most people report that their hands are hot or tingling when they channel and the recipient is usually also aware of a warmth coming from the practitioner's hands. However it must be stressed that there is no right sensation here and everyone experiences the energy a little differently. Sometimes (unusually) the heat is intense, causing practitioners to break out in a sweat, sometimes it's like having feathers rolled against your palms. The first time I felt Reiki energy I remember describing it as being like putting my hands in fizzy water, with lots of little bubbles popping on my palms. Afterwards the person I was practicing with said "Reiki's lovely, your hands are as warm as toast!"

If I don't feel anything has it not worked for me?

Although the majority of practitioners feel something, these sensations aren't a necessary part of the healing. Even if you feel nothing at all the Reiki hasn't 'misfired' and you aren't immune to the energy, as some students imagine. Once you are attuned you are a Reiki channel and you can heal regardless of the sensations in your hands. So don't get discouraged.

After the attunements

In order for the Reiki energy to become a part of your life tradition tells us that a newly attuned practitioner should practice a period of self healing everyday for twenty-one days. It is sometimes said that the Reiki energy rises up from chakra to chakra, dwelling at each in turn for three days, and so taking twenty-one days to move through all seven.

Whether or not this is the case twenty-one days should be enough time to thoroughly embed a regular Reiki practice into your life and make it a part of you. As such it is a tradition and discipline well worth embracing.

You can work intuitively or follow set hand positions as you feel guided to do.

What about the 21 day cleanse / healing crisis?

Although there are usually no side effects to Reiki treatments other than the immediate heat, light and sound described above there can be more concrete side effects following on from the Reiki I attunements.

A process sometimes known as the *21 day cleanse* or the healing crisis is often discussed on Reiki courses with Reiki masters differing as to whether they believe the effects to by psycho-somatic (we discuss a 'healing crisis' so you imagine you're having one) or very genuine with symptoms rising up the body as the energy makes it way from the base of the spine to the crown of the head.

Personally I have no firm views, but it is noticeable that many new practitioners do find that they suddenly develop a cold or a runny nose, may feel headachy or tired and are puzzled that their new found healing ability seems to have made them ill.

If these mild illnesses happen to you don't worry, just continue to self treat and you will find that you pass through your symptoms faster than you would normally.

Note: If you have symptoms of a severe or worrying nature please do consult a medical doctor, having been attuned to Reiki won't have caused this, but it won't immediately prevent you from contracting something serious either and you must use your common sense.

Becoming a hollow bamboo

At this stage in your Reiki journey you've learned something about Reiki history (sources of further information are given at the end of this book), you've experienced the attunements and you've practiced giving and receiving Reiki energy. You've embarked on a wonderful and productive path that can benefit both you and those you treat in host of different ways.

Although the Reiki energy is now yours for life it's a good practice to keep working with the energy, and your capacity to channel it, in order to deepen your connection and make yourself a clear channel for the Reiki to flow through. This capacity to channel energy is often likened to being a 'hollow bamboo', you become a channel through which energy flows and the more open and uncluttered the channel is the faster and more easily the energy will flow.

We'll look now at a series of techniques that help to clear away some of the energetic debris that collects around us in our day-to-day lives before progressing to a method of that increases the energy flow and our healing potential.

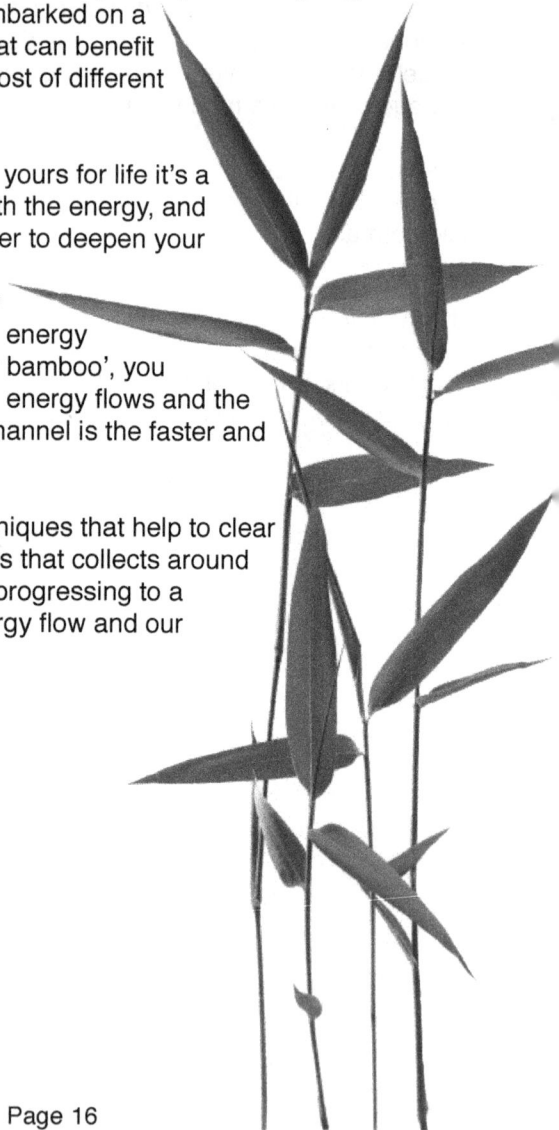

Gassho Meditation

The simple mediation below trains your mind to meditate peacefully by using the sensations you find in your body.

How often should I use this technique?

It's a good idea to begin with no more than five minute sessions of mediation, building up to 20-30 minutes a day if possible.

1. Make your body comfortable, kneeling, sitting or standing. The traditional posture for this meditation is kneeling with the knees and feet together, sat back on your heels, but this can become uncomfortable very quickly if you're not used to it. Remember that *gassho* meditation should always be gentle, never an attempt to endure painful limbs.

2. Close your eyes and bring your palms together at heart level.

3. Concentrate on the tiny area where the pads of your middle two fingers touch. Rest your attention wholly in the sensations you have between these fingers.

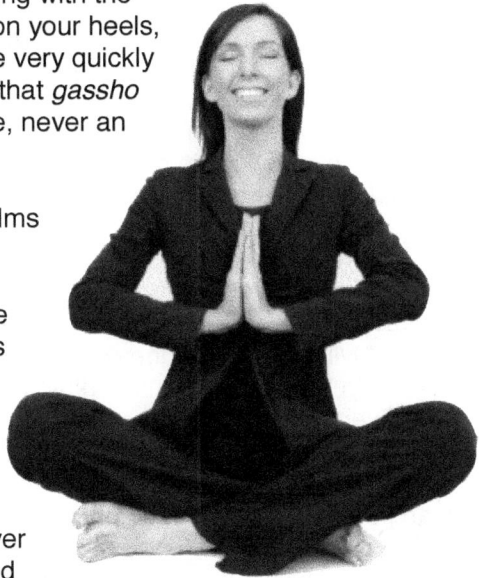

You may find that this is not as easy as it sounds, particularly if you've never meditated before. If you find your mind wandering, even after a few seconds, just gently bring it back to the sensation. It's important not to be harsh or judgmental with yourself about your wandering thoughts, just notice that they've moved on and go back to the finger tips.

As you remain in *gassho*, simply letting your thoughts go past, you're cultivating your inner stillness. As you continue this practice through the weeks and months you'll begin to notice that you can carry this stillness with you when conducting treatments and your ability to steady your mind and pick-up on the signals from your hands and other senses will increase.

Reciting the Reiki Principles

Many Reiki practitioners start the day with a recitation of the Reiki Principles. Repetition of the Principles was one of the original teachings of the founder who advised us:

> *"Every morning and evening join your hands and say these words to your heart and chant these words [the Reiki principles] with your mouth."*

So how can this practice help us become better Reiki channels?

As we found when we experienced *gassho* mediation a mind that is still and clear is a mind that receives what's around it with greater accuracy, empathy and understanding. If we have minds that are clouded with anger, worry, selfishness, dishonesty and meanness we have very little space left to offer the altruistic gift of Reiki, even to ourselves. The recitation of the principles, coupled with a sincere attempt to live them, frees us from the burden of living with a mind weighed down by the negative emotions they seek to free us from.

However, if we look at the principles we can become afraid: "I will not be angry, I will not worry..." they seem like almost impossible goals. So Usui-sensei, in his wisdom, removed most of this burden from us: We don't say "I will never be angry again", a seemingly impossible task, we say every morning "Just for today, I will not be angry" and so we can give ourselves the freedom to change tomorrow, we can acknowledge that we are less than perfect and still aim high, just for today.

If we fail, if we become angry, if we worry, if we are dishonest, unkind or ungrateful we can start again tomorrow. Reiki is a forgiving path that allows us to grow and renew and does not judge us.

So, every morning, whether you go on to the full *gassho* meditation or not, take a little quiet time, put your hands together and repeat to your self three times with as much determination as you can:

> *"Just for today, I will not be angry, I will not worry, I will be grateful, I will work honestly and I will be kind to every living thing."*

Joshin kokyuu-ho: Cleansing Breath

Now that we've learned to still the mind with the *gassho* mediation and learned the value of a daily commitment to keeping our minds free of negative emotions it's time to begin the process of working with the Reiki energy. The Cleansing Breath, *Joshin kokyuu-ho*, is used to help you connect to the energy and let it move through you, clearing your energy and dissolving blockages.

How often should I use this technique?

Personally I love this exercise so I use it everyday as part of my morning Reiki routine, but you can use it as often as you feel you want to, either making it a regular part of your practice or using it from time to time to help you refresh if you've not practiced in a while.

Please note: This exercise should not be used by anyone with high blood pressure or at any time during pregnancy. Please stop the exercise if you find yourself becoming light headed.

Joshin kokyuu-ho can be performed in any position where you can have a straight back. Sitting, standing, kneeling or in your favourite meditation posture are all fine.

1. Inhale through your nose and draw Reiki in through the crown of your head. To increase your connection you can visualise the energy as a benevolent white light pouring into you through the top of your head.

2. Consciously pull the energy down through your body into your *tanden* and collect it there. (The *tanden* is located three finger-widths below the navel, on the midline, about a third of the way into your body).

The Tanden
(Dantien)

3. Pause for a few seconds and consciously radiate the energy through out your body, reaching every part, but not yet passing beyond you. Again you can intensify this be visualising the white light spreading throughout you, filling you, and pushing all the spiritual debris out of your body.

4. Exhale through your mouth and flow the energy out through your fingertips, palms, the tips of your toes and the soles of your feet.

   In this part of the exercise you are becoming a channel for the Reiki and directing it consciously with your intention.

   This is good practice for giving physical treatments at this level of training and to prepare for giving distant healing at level II.

Hatsu Rei Ho

Hatsu Rei Ho is actually a collection of several techniques, including the *gassho* mediation above, each of which can be practiced on its own if desired. It builds on the visualisation skills you've practiced with *Joshin kokyuu ho* and consists of six stages.

How often should I use this technique?

The practice of *Hatsu Rei Ho*, or *Reiki Starting Technique*, can be used daily or weekly to increase your connection to Reiki, your ability to sense its movements and to clear your energetic blocks.

Focusing

1. Sit down in a comfortable position with your hands on your knees, palms down.
2. Focus on your *tanden* (also called the *dantien*, located 2-3 finger-widths under your bellybutton and about a third of the way into your body.)
3. Fix your intention to practice *Hatsu Rei Ho*.

Kenyoku (brushing off)

1. Place your right hand flat on your left collar bone.
2. Sweep your hand down and across your body, ending at your right hip, exhaling as you do so.
3. Repeat on the opposite side.
4. Repeat on the first side. You will now have used right hand, left hand, right hand.
5. Extend your left arm in front of you so that it's away from the body with the finger tips at hip height.
6. Place your right hand on your left shoulder.
7. Sweep your right hand down your left arm and past the finger tips, exhaling as you do so.
8. Repeat on the other side
9. Repeat on the first side. You will now have used right hand, left hand, right hand as before.

Connection

1. Raise your arms above your head, palms upward, elbows soft with the finger tips facing into your crown about 10cm apart.
2. Make the connection to Reiki by visualising a soft white light pouring into your palm chakras and flowing down your arms and into your body.
3. Feel the energy flowing. When you become fully aware of the flow gently lower your arms to rest again, palms down, on your knees.

Gassho

1. Hold your hands together in the *gassho* position with the palms opposite your heart.
2. Bring your attention to the tiny area where the pads of your middle two fingers touch.
3. Hold your attention there for as long as it will remain without causing tension.

Seishin Toitsu (My spirit is gathered)

1. With your hands still in *gassho* breathe in and experience light pouring into your hands and flowing down to your *tanden* and building there.
2. Breathe out and experience the light moving back up and pouring out of your hands.

Returning

1. Return your hands to their starting position, palms down on your knees.
2. Acknowledge to yourself that you have finished *Hatsu Rei Ho*
3. Return to the everyday world by shaking your hands out and returning your mind to your surroundings.

Active working

The type of practices we've experienced so far underpin a commitment to becoming an effective Reiki practitioner and I hope you've begun to notice the changes. Although it is possible to practice Reiki without ever undertaking these steps your ability to heal and your own personal growth will be vastly improved by making a commitment to become a 'hollow bamboo' for the energy to flow through.

Once you've practiced the *gassho* meditation for a while and you've learnt the value of visualising the energy in *joshin kokyuu ho* and *hatsu rei ho* you'll have realised how powerful your focused intent can be.

When you pull the energy down into your *tanden* in *joshin kokyuu ho* you're using your mind to say "energy flow here" and it does. When you visualise the energy flowing into your upraised palms in *hatsu rei ho*, it does and you feel it.

It's often said in Reiki circles that energy follows thought. I hope that you've now experienced this for yourself and you're ready to apply it when giving Reiki treatments and self-healing.

How often should I use this technique?

At Reiki I you should use this technique as often as possible when giving Reiki or self-healing. If you find your mind wandering or you simply forget to use it don't worry, the Reiki still flows, but using an active working technique increases the flow of energy and your ability to be an effective healer.

We'll go into the various methods for determining which areas of the body to work on later on in this book so for now we'll just look at how to use visualisaion to direct the energy when you have your hands over an area you want to treat:

1. With your hands either on or over the area you're going to treat begin to visualise the pure Reiki energy as a brilliant white light directly above your head.

2. Breathe in and consciously draw the energy down through the crown of your head, through the middle of your body, to your *tanden*.

3. Breathe out and send the energy up from your *tanden*, out through your palms and into the area you're treating.

4. Try to visualise the energy actually permeating the area under your hands and flooding it with beneficial energy.

5. Repeat steps 2-4 on each breath whilst your hands are in position.

Supporting practices

As well as the energy exercises detailed above there are other ways to improve your appreciation and understanding of Reiki:

Journaling
After a treatment session, either on yourself or someone else, make a note of what your felt and thought in a book set aside for that purpose.

Over time your Reiki journal will help you to discover the meaning of the particular sensations and feelings you have when giving treatments and how you can use them to better understand your own and others' needs.

If you have sensations of heat, tingling, pulsing or coldness in your hands, or have feelings of pressure or sense colours or lights when working with Reiki these sensations will have a unique meaning for you. You can discover these meanings by performing regular treatments, particularly self-healing at this level, and writing them down. Over time you'll learn to notice that particular sensations occur before you come down with a cold, that a particular sensation always occurs when treating a friend with indigestion and so on.

It can be hard to remember exactly what you felt on each occasion if you don't record it in some way, so your Reiki journal can prove one of your biggest assets in developing your sensitivity.

Reiki Shares

Reiki shares are regular, usually monthly, meetings organised by a Reiki master. The meeting will usually involve some form of group energy exercise, possibly a *Reiju* empowerment and followed by treatments (either only in the group or with members of the public) and ending with a discussion about how everyone feels they are progressing in Reiki.

Reiki shares are good ways to get feedback, receive Reiki and share your gift with others.

Fun stuff

Although not strictly part of Reiki training it can be helpful and fun try Reiki experiments with your food, drink, plants and surroundings:

1. Try giving Reiki to your pot plants by holding your hands around the base. If you have two similar plants try giving Reiki to one and not the other, how do the two compare?

2. When you pour a glass of water try giving it Reiki. Does it alter the taste? You can try this with any kind of food or drink and it's even been said to improve the flavour of cheep wine!

3. Try giving your house a Reiki spring clean - stand in the middle of each room and perform *joshin kokyuu ho*, but this time sending the energy out in to the room and visualise it cleansing the atmosphere of all negative vibrations.

If you find any interesting results remember to write them down in your journal.

Giving a treatment

Preparation: the environment

A Reiki treatment should be a sacred time and treated with respect. You are going to heal yourself or another human being, who will benefit not only from the energy but from time to rest and relax and receive the healing.

If it's possible set a relaxing atmosphere for the treatment. This could involve relaxing music, gentle scents such as incense or essential oils and ambient lighting that avoids directly shining in the eyes.

If the recipient is going to be treated lying down on a massage table, bed or floor make sure that you have blankets and pillows to hands so they can make themselves comfortable and keep warm whilst lying still.

Preparation: yourself

Before beginning the treatment stand or kneel at the head of the recipient and spend a little time in the *gassho* meditation given in the previous chapter.

When you feel you have achieved some measure of inner stillness it's time to connect to the energy. Many people do this through the use of a phrase or statement such as the simple words "Reiki on", others use a small prayer or invocation. I use the phrase "Let the Reiki flow". It's the first thing that occurred to me when my teacher said it was a good idea to have a verbal trigger to let myself know I'd begun and it's stuck with me ever since.

Once you've made the connection to the energy it's time to set your intention. Once again the words or images you choose should be the things that seem best to you but now they must focus on carrying out the treatment for the highest good of the recipient. Here I use the rather conventional "for the highest good of [the recipient] and all sentient beings".

Release your hands from the *gassho* when you feel ready, there is no fixed time for this, but remember that you have a recipient who is waiting for you to begin.

About your hands

There are a few important things to remember about your hands when giving Reiki:

1. **Keep them loose**. Make sure that your hands, wrists, elbows and shoulders are in a relaxed state. This not only helps the energy to flow freely but makes sure that you won't get muscle cramps from holding yourself in too rigid a position.

2. **Keep your fingers together**. The four fingers on each hand should be touching one another at all times when giving Reiki (Unless forming a Reiki pointer, you'll learn about that at Reiki II).

    However, you can move your thumb away if that would be more comfortable in some positions (e.g. under the head).

3. **You can stack them**. If you feel a small area needs all your attention you can place one hand over the other and channel through both of them. This increases the amount of energy available to an area and can prove very effective.

    I use this technique when dealing with the kind of migraine that only affects one side of the face or with dental pain for example.

Beginning the treatment

Once you have fixed your intention there are two ways of beginning a Reiki treatment, either moving directly to the first of the hand positions or using intuitive working to locate areas directly in need of energy. Both hand positions and intuitive working are covered in turn here and only time spent tuning into your intuition will tell you which is right for you at any given time.

Hand positions

The first thing to say about hand positions is that there is a lot of variation in their number and placement taught by Reiki masters.

It is now thought that Usui-sensei used five basic hand positions before going on to use *Reiji Ho* (covered later); Dr. Hyashi is reported to have used seven and those working in his clinic used twelve. Today you will find some Reiki masters teaching over twenty positions and it can be confusing for the novice practitioner.

Set hand positions are an important part of the first Reiki level as it takes practice to learn to listen to the sensations in your hands and then finally to use your intuition. The hand positions are a method that let you practice Reiki, work with the energy and build up your experience.

The following set of hand positions ensures that the whole body is treated and will help you to build up your experience. If you find that you are comfortable with the rhythm of using set hand positions and never feel moved to try the intuitive methods that's fine. There is nothing substandard about this and you are still a true Reiki channel.
The second thing to say about hand positions is to do with the way the recipient is lying. It has been traditional in the West to ask a recipient to turn over so that you can work on their back a little over half way through the treatment.

Experience tells us that this can break up the relaxing effects of the treatment for the recipient and some people find lying on their front uncomfortable or embarrassing. In light of this I would not recommend asking people to turn over during this full-body style of treatment and the hand positions given below are for front treatment only.

If you are wondering how to treat someone with a specific back or kidney problem then I would always advise you treat that area directly before beginning a full-body treatment, trying to sense how long you should remain. As Usui-sensei said:

> "If a brain disease occurs, I treat the head. If it's a stomachache, I treat the stomach. If it's an eye disease, I treat the eyes."

So if you are presented with a specific problem always treat that directly first. Hand positions for specific areas and conditions are given in the translation of the *Reiki Ryoho Hikkei* that accompanies this guide.

1. The eyes
Standing at the head of the recipient hold both hands side-by-side, thumbs touching, hands a little cupped. Hold the two hands together over the face so your palms are over their eyes.

You can hover the hands or place them gently as seems best to you, but do not use pressure and most importantly, however tired your arms feel, do not lean on the recipient!

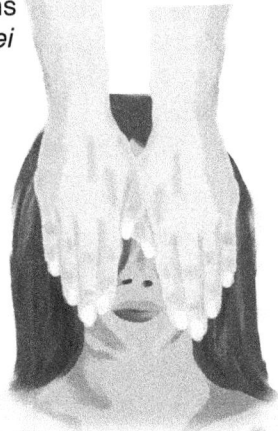

2. The sides of the face
Keeping your hands cupped remove them from the eyes and place them over the ears and against the side of the face.

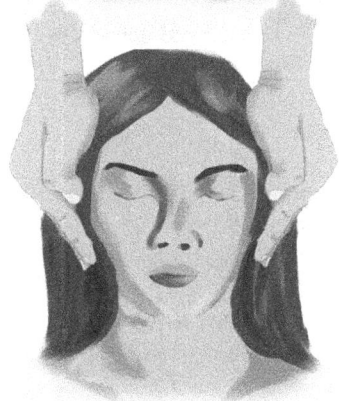

3. The back of the head
This position takes care to get into as we do not want to disturb the recipient too much.

Place your hands, palms flat. against the sides of the recipient's head towards the crown. Roll their head gently to one side, not letting it fall, and slide the opposite hand underneath.

Using your other hand roll the head gently back the other side, sliding your second hand underneath and return the head to centre. Reverse this process to come out of the position.

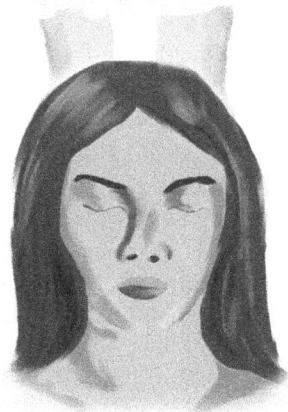

4. Throat

Still at the head place the hands in a 'v' shape with fingertips touching just in front of the throat. This is a very vulnerable area of the body and there must be no pressure used at all. Many practitioners find it best to hover the hands slightly in this positions so that is no chance of the recipient feeling choked or nervous.

5. Centre of the chest

Move around to the side of the recipient and place your hands, again next to one another, in the centre of the chest at heart level. If the recipient is a woman it is not acceptable to place your hands directly on her body in this area. As with the throat position float the hands 2-3cm above the body.

6. The solar plexus

This is the area midway between the waist and the bottom of the ribcage and is located on the midline.

Hands can be placed next to one another as before or can be chained with the the heal of one hand touching the fingertips of the other.

7. Sacral area

This is the area also known as the *tanden*, *dantien*, sacral chakra or *hara*. It is located 2-3 finger widths below the naval and again rests on the midline. Hands are placed as with the solar plexus.

8. Groin

Stand to the side of the recipient facing towards their head. Make your hands in to a 'v' shape with the heals of the hands touching.

Hover the hands about 2-3 cm above the recipient with the fingertips at the level of the hipbones. Once again this is a sensitive area and should not be touched directly.

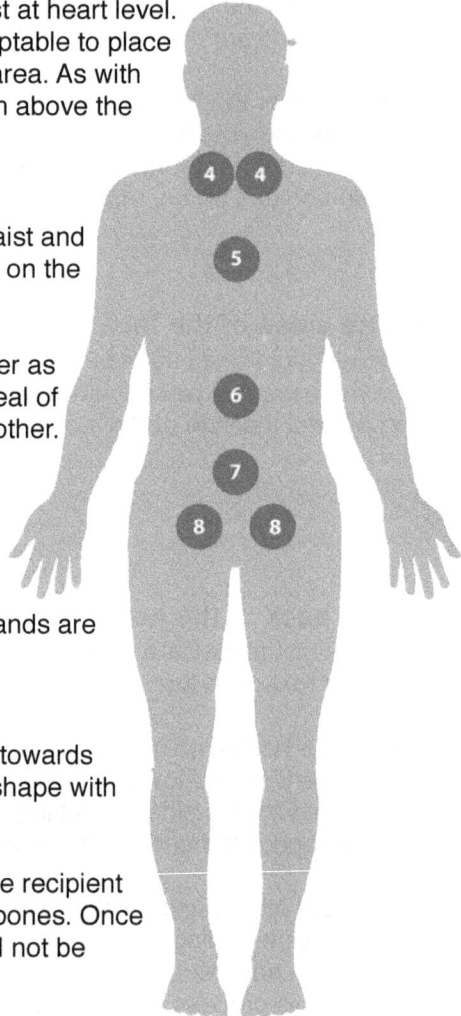

9. Legs and ankles

Standing next to the middle of the lower leg place one hand on the knee joint and one on the ankle joint. Repeat on the other side.

10. Feet

Stand facing the soles of the recipient's feet.

Hold the foot between your hands with your palms opposite the centre of the foot and at right angles to it. Repeat on the other side.

Returning

As Reiki can be a profoundly relaxing experience for the recipient it's a good idea to have a short technique to bring them gently back into the everyday world. My *Shoden* teacher taught me the technique of gently running the heal of my right hand down the sole of the foot two or three times with a gentle but firm pressure. As this is different to anything that has happened so far it gently stimulates the recipient's mind and begins to bring them back.

You can then go back to their shoulder level and tell them that you'll be leaving the room to get them a drink of water and will return in a few minutes. This gives them a little privacy to get up and 'come around' in their own time.

A drink of water is also traditionally offered at this time to complete the cleansing aspects of the treatment.

Intuitive working

There are two main types of intuitive working that grow naturally out using Reiki: *Byosen reikan ho* and *Reiji ho*. As we discussed in class you should use *Byosen reikan ho* until you have worked with the energy for some time and have grown used to listening to it intuitively.

Byosen Reikan Ho
This technique involves scanning the body for *byosen* or areas of blocked energy and then treating each area individually.

After the *gassho* instead of moving to the first hand position we float the hands about 2-3cm from the body and move them in slow sweeping movements. When we do this we are using the sensations in our hands and minds to sense *byosen*, the areas of illness, potential illness and blocked energy in the recipient.

When we encounter a *byosen* we feel sensations known as *hibiki* and this alerts us that the area our hands are over is in need of healing. The *hibiki* sensation takes a wide variety of forms from increased heat, chill, vibration or just a strong sense that our hands should remain where they are.

Although the first instance of *hibiki* may move you to instantly treat the area it's important to scan the whole body first incase there is a more pressing need elsewhere. You may not have enough time to throughly treat every *byosen* so it's important to be aware of them all when using this technique.

Reiji Ho
This technique is a little more advanced than *Byosen reikan ho* as it involves working intuitively rather than finding *hibiki* with our hands.

After *gassho* take a moment to listen to your intuition and where it's telling you to go. You may find that your hands are pulled to, or float to, a particular area of the recipients body and that they remain there until pulled to another place.

Let your hands work as the energy guides them, not trying to work out why they are there or worrying about where you should go next.

As you can see this differs from *Byosen reikan ho* in that we are not looking for areas of the body that cause *hibiki* and thinking about which to treat, we are placing ourselves totally at the disposal of the energy and going where it prompts us.

For both methods it is good once again to carry out the little 'returning ritual' given in the hand positions section as a good way to bring the recipient back into full consciousness.

Self Healing

One of the most useful things you can do to develop your sensitivity and clear yourself to channel is to perform regular self-treatments. There are several methods for this and you may find that you use different ones at different times:

- **Hand positions**: you can adapt the hand positions given above for self-treatment with very little difficulty. You can work sitting down, kneeling or lying depending on your preference. If you choose to lie down it can be a good idea to keep a couple of cushions handy to put under your elbows, if you need to stack both hands over your heart centre, tanden or brow it can get tiring to keep your arms up without support.

- **Intuitive working**: begin with a *gassho* meditation to still your mind. When you're ready to begin turn your attention away from your finger tips and let it rest gently on the whole of your body. If you're going to progress using *byosen reikan ho* slowly lift your hands to your forehead and run them down along your torso, ending at the *tanden*. Pause a moment and if required run the hands down from the *tanden* to the lower legs and feet. Note any instances of *hibiki* and move on to treat them accordingly.

  If using *reiji ho* remain in the *gassho* posture without moving your hands. As before turn your attention from the fingertips to the whole body. Remain in an open, receptive state until you receive an intuition about where to treat.

Ethics & permission

There are a few ethical guidelines that every Reiki practitioner must respect, if only for their safety in these litigious times.

At Reiki I these guidelines assume that you are not in a professional practice but treating family, friends and others at meetings such as Reiki shares.

If you need a full set of guidelines for professional practice I recommend that you consult the Reiki Federation who have extensive resources for professionals: www.reikifed.co.uk

Dignity and privacy
- Don't begin a treatment until you have the definite permission of the recipient.
- Don't lay hands on any personal areas of the body such as the groin or breasts, always hold your hands 2-3cm away.
- Don't dictate what the recipient should ware for a treatment other than the general guideline that it should be comfortable and preferably loose.

Your relationship to the medical profession
- Never offer a medical opinion or try to diagnose an illness.
- Never contradict or cast doubt on the the opinion of a recipient's doctor or medical advisors.
- Never promise or guarantee healing.
- If you become convinced that there is an issue that requires a physician then tell the recipient that you sense a particular imbalance and that they may like to see a doctor. Never insist that they go and don't frighten them.

A Reiki week

Developing a daily routine of meditation and self healing as well as incorporating some of the energy exercises on a weekly basis can be a powerful way to increase your capacity to channel Reiki and your sensitivity to the energy.

The following is a guideline plan for a 'Reiki week' to give you an idea how you might go about doing this:

Daily practice

- In the morning, as soon as you can after rising (really difficult for those of us with small children I know!) take a moment to stand or sit in *gassho* and recite the Reiki principles three times with as much attention and understanding as you can.

- Take 15 - 20 minutes of quite time during the day to make the *gassho* meditation (p.18) If this can follow on from the recitation of the principles that would be ideal but if that isn't practical for you fit it in as best you can.

- Optional: Finish your *gassho* with 5 minutes of *joshin kokyuu-ho* (p. 19).

- Before bed (if that suits your routines) take 10 - 20 minutes to practice self-healing. If you're currently using hand positions try working on your intuition by experimenting with *byosen reikan ho*.

Weekly practice

- Incorporate *hatsu rei ho* (p. 22) into your daily routine on one day each week. If you're pressured for time you can use this to replace your daily *joshin kokyuu ho*.

- Try to give Reiki to someone else, even if only for 5 - 10 minutes, at least once a week. This gives you valuable practice in learning to listen to your intuition and the feedback you get from your senses.

- Write up your Reiki journal. Every time you self-treat, give Reiki or experience anything in meditation make a note of it in your journal. It's going to be one of your best teachers, I promise you.

This 'Reiki week' incorporates a daily practice of about 30 - 40 minutes across two sessions and is intended as a guideline to help you plan your own routines.

Please don't get discouraged if this seems like a lot, if you can incorporate meditation, self-healing and practice into your life in any way you're going to progress in Reiki and ultimately a system that's tailored to your life is the one that's going to work best for you. So be inventive with your practice, there's nothing to stop you self-healing on the bus!

Your Reiki Lineage

As Reiki is passed from Master to student by direct transmission it is customary for Reiki practitioners to know and pass on their lineage. My Reiki lineage is given on the next page with space for you to add your name. Please feel free to copy the diagram if you'd like to.

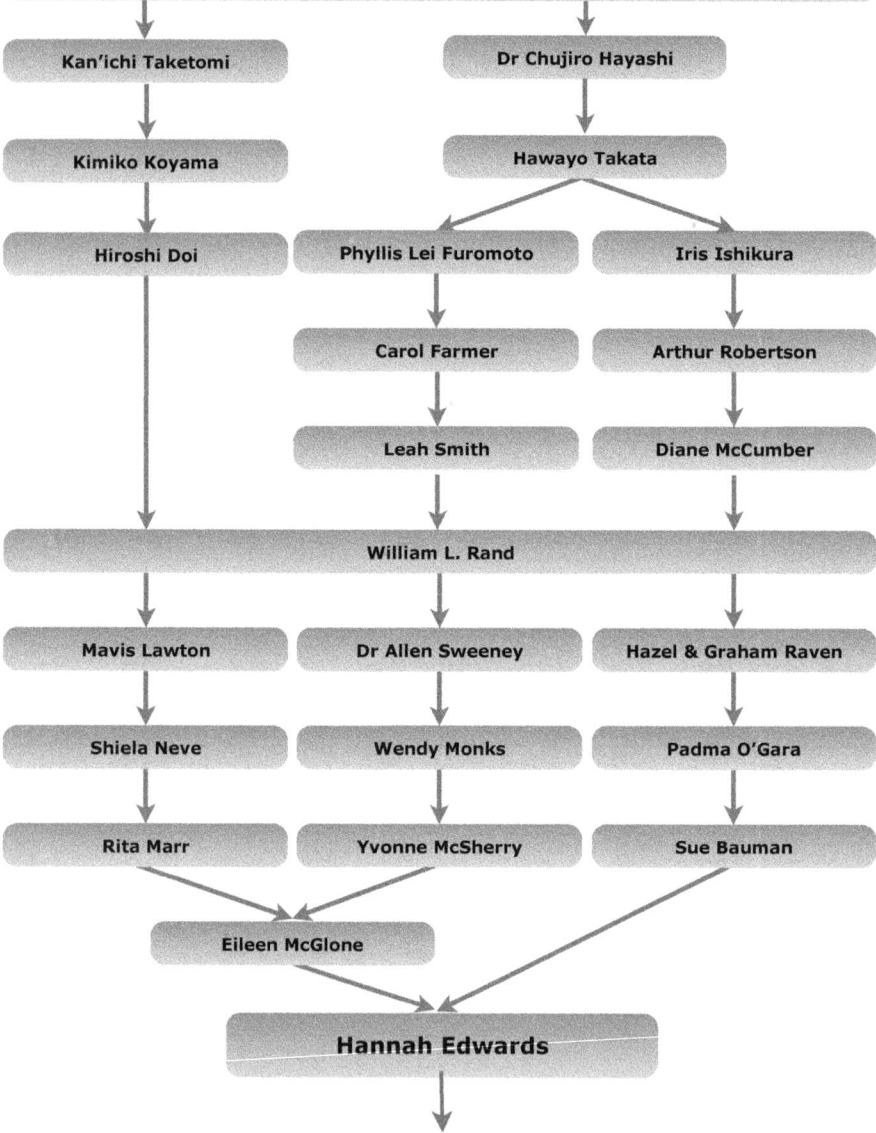

Mikao Usui

Kan'ichi Taketomi

Dr Chujiro Hayashi

Kimiko Koyama

Hawayo Takata

Hiroshi Doi

Phyllis Lei Furomoto

Iris Ishikura

Carol Farmer

Arthur Robertson

Leah Smith

Diane McCumber

William L. Rand

Mavis Lawton

Dr Allen Sweeney

Hazel & Graham Raven

Shiela Neve

Wendy Monks

Padma O'Gara

Rita Marr

Yvonne McSherry

Sue Bauman

Eileen McGlone

Hannah Edwards

Glossary

Byosen	Areas of blocked energy or pre-illness which can be detected and treated through *byosen reikan ho*.
Channeling	In energy work: The process of consciously directing energy through the body and into a recipient, object or body part. In spiritualism: The process of communicating with spirit guides or the deceased.
Gassho	Lit. Japanese: Two hands coming together. *Gassho* refers to the 'prayer' mudra in which the hands are placed, palms together in front of the heart.
Hibbiki	The sensations felt in the hands when they encounter a *bysoen* in *byosen reikan ho*.
Reiju	The empowerment or blessing, without symbols, used by Usui-sensei to pass on Reiki.
Tanden	The area approximately three fingers below the navel on the midline and about a third of the way into the body. This area is a major energy centre and is used to store and distribute energy in many spiritual traditions.
Usui Shiki Ryoho	This refers to Reiki in the Hayashi-Takata lineage. The hallmarks of this system are the use of symbol based attunements and a heavy emphasis on the importance of the Reiki symbols at levels II and above.
Usui Reiki Ryoho	This refers to the original practice of Reiki as taught by Usui-sensei and still practiced in Japan.

Further Information

I hope that you have enjoyed your time with Reiki and will want to make it a permanent part of your life. To help you develop your practice here are a few suggestions for further reading and support.

Books

The Original Reiki Handbook of Dr. Mikao Usui
Mikao Usui & Frank Arjava Petter

ISBN: 978-0914955573

This slim volume (80 pages) gives the practical sections from the original notes of Mikao Usui illustrated with modern photographs of the hand positions for specific ailments.

Reiki Fire - New information about the origins of the Reiki power.
Frank Arjava Petter

ISBN: 978-0914955504

Following five years of research in Japan Frank Arjava Petter has complied a book that sheds a great deal of light on the mysterious origins of Reiki and the personalities behind its growth.

The Spirit of Reiki
Walter Lubeck, Frank Arjava Petter & William Lee Rand

ISBN: 81-7769-124-4

Written by three well known Reiki masters from different traditions this book looks at a diverse range of Reiki topics including Reiki history, treatment positions and the Hyashi Healing Guide.

Hands of Light: A Guide to Healing Through the Human Energy Field
Barbara Anne Brennan

ISBN: 978-0553345391

Although not a guide to Reiki as such this classic guide to energy healing will appeal to you if you are interested the wider world of auric and chakra healing.

Associations

The UK Reiki Federation

www.reikifed.co.uk

The UK Reiki Federation is the main professional body for Reiki practitioners in the UK and provides affordable practice insurance as well as a wealth of resources including magazines, leaflets, practice guidelines, a member's register and even branded clothing.

The Reiki Association

www.reikiassociation.org.uk

The Reiki Association offers people who have Reiki the opportunity to be in community together and membership is open to anyone attuned to Reiki. The Reiki Association differs from the Reiki Federation in that membership is not graded by your degree and the emphasis is on personal rather than professional development.

Thank you

I'd like to take this opportunity to thank your for studying with me and wish you all the best in your work with Reiki, I hope you find it as rewarding a path as I have.

Blessings,
Hannah

www.reiki-with-hannah.co.uk